WHAT IS A CAT?

WHAT IS A ?

For Everyone Who Has Ever Loved a Cat

BILL ADLER

Illustrations by Douglas Florian

WILLIAM MORROW AND COMPANY, INC. / NEW YORK

Library of Congress Cataloging-in-Publication Data

Adler, Bill.
  What is a cat?

  1. Anecdotes, facetiae, satire, etc.   2. Cats —
Caricatures and cartoons.   I. Florian, Douglas.
II. Title.
PN6231.C23A34 1987   741.5′973   87–12376
ISBN 0-688-07528-2

Printed in the United States of America

First Edition

1 2 3 4 5 6 7 8 9 10

BOOK DESIGN BY RICHARD ORIOLO

To everyone
who has ever loved a cat,
this book is for you.

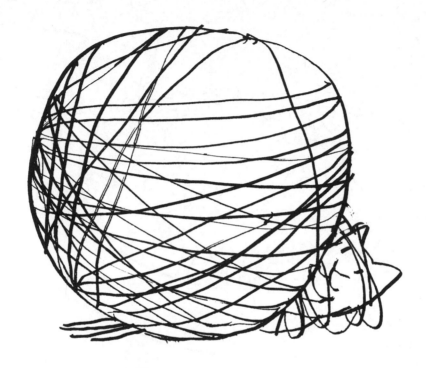

A cat is someone
who can be happy with just a
ball of string.

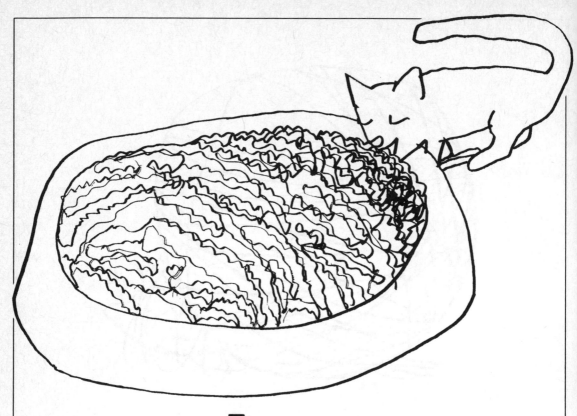

A cat can eat
one meal a day—all day.

A cat is
someone with sharp front claws.
Ask anyone with new furniture.

A cat lets the dog be
man's best friend because she doesn't
want the responsibility.

A cat is love!

A cat will purr
when she is happy, meow when she is sad, and be
silent when she is planning
her next move.

A cat doesn't
do tricks. She leaves that to the
"big cats" in the circus.

A cat may come when
you call her—if she doesn't have
something better to do.

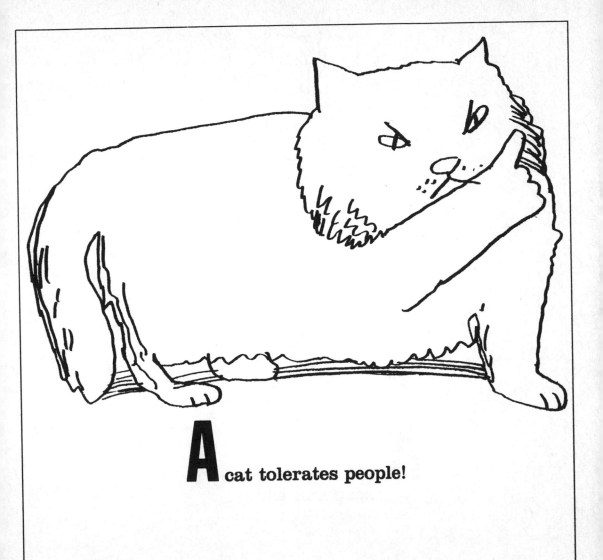

A cat tolerates people!

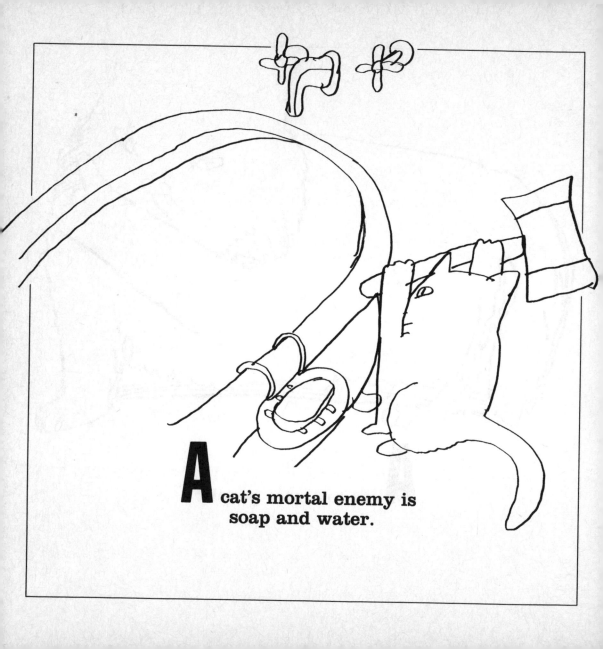

A cat's mortal enemy is
soap and water.

A cat is curious
about everything except big dogs.

A cat can lower
your blood pressure just by
sitting on your lap.

A cat knows that
cats are very popular but can't
figure out why!

A cat has nine lives
because she doesn't take chances.

A cat living in Paris speaks
fluent French.

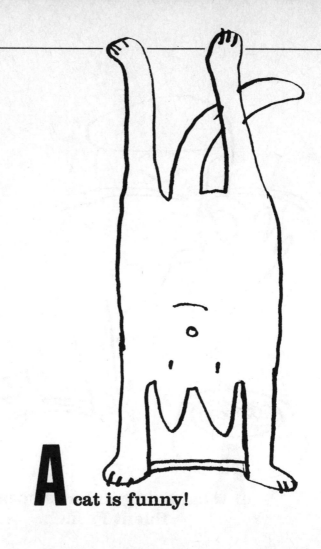

A cat is funny!

A cat always lands
on her feet.

A cat can't
understand why all the fuss
about teddy bears.

A cat never
lets a black cat cross in
front of her.

A cat can usually
be found where you don't expect
her to be.

A cat is purr-fect!

A cat never
reveals what she is thinking.

A cat thinks
people make great pets.

A cat is special!

A cat who
lives in Russia is a Communist.

A cat has feelings.

A cat doesn't
care how rich or famous you are.

A cat would
prefer not to go to a cat show.

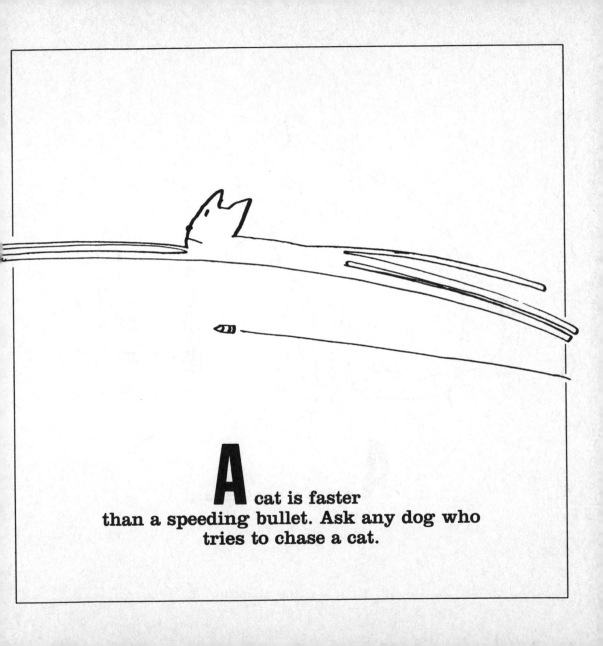

A cat is faster
than a speeding bullet. Ask any dog who
tries to chase a cat.

A cat is a neat freak!

A cat isn't perfect—but don't tell that to your cat.

A cat is her own best friend.

A cat tolerates kittens.

A cat can't read
the label on a can of cat food but still
knows what is in the can.

A cat thinks books about
cats are silly.

A cat is hugs.

A cat doesn't mess
in politics and family fights.

A cat is sick of
people who call every cat "Tabby."

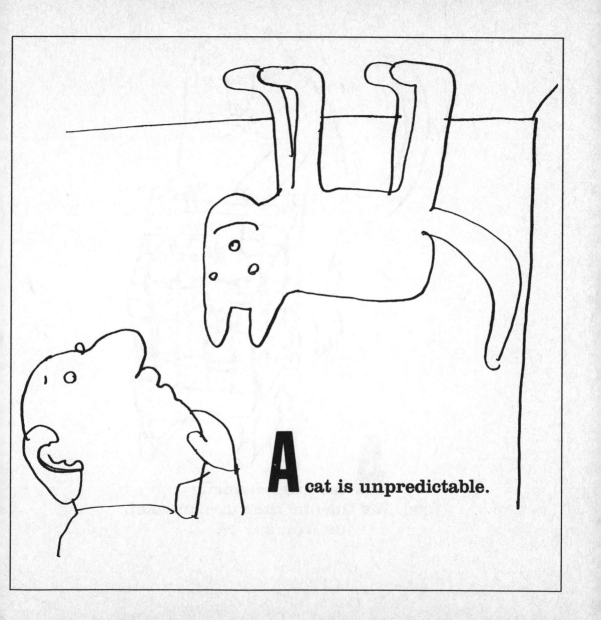

A cat is unpredictable.

A cat has a favorite
food. It's the one the supermarket
just ran out of.

A cat's litter box is her castle.

A cat never lets you down.

A cat is your friend forever.

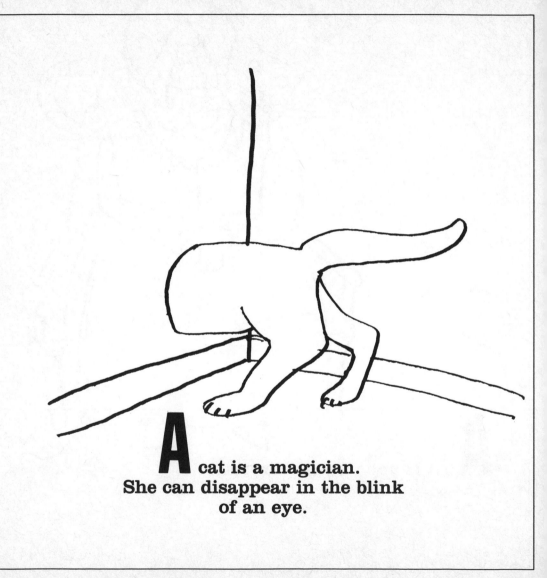

A cat is a magician.
She can disappear in the blink
of an eye.

A cat's favorite
place to sleep is your favorite
place to sleep.

A cat has an
innocent face and a cunning mind.

A cat is moody.

A cat is a great actor.

A cat has
perfect hearing—except when you
call her.

A cat is cool!

A cat is strong.
Just ask anyone who has tried to get her
down from a ledge.

A cat with her
tail up has something on her mind.

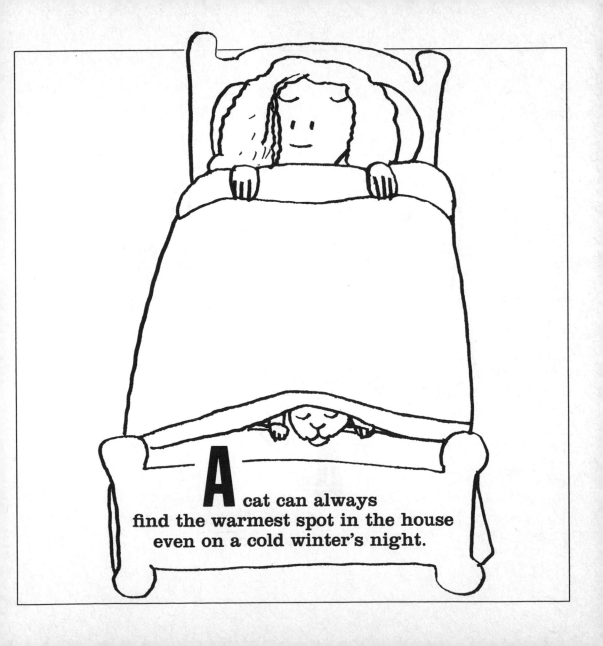

A cat can always
find the warmest spot in the house
even on a cold winter's night.

A cat can
entertain you for hours even if she
doesn't do tricks.

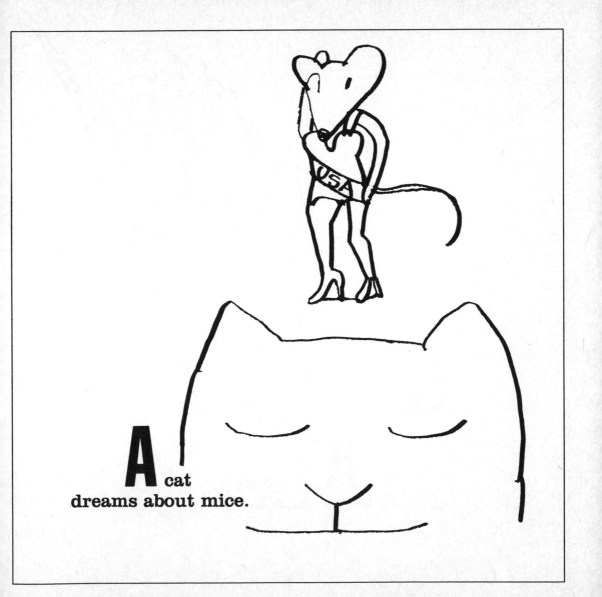

A cat
dreams about mice.

A cat's hiss
is worse than her bite.

A cat can become
invisible when she knows you are
looking for her.

A cat meows when she is hungry,
purrs when she is happy, and says nothing
when you want to know who
broke the vase.